# WHAT HAPPENS
# WHEN WOMEN
## *Converge*

**How REVERENT Engagement Unearths
the POTENCY of the Collective FEMININE**

❧ by Patricia Fero ❧

For information address Healing Dynamics Inc. 3013
Williamsburg, Ann Arbor, Mi. 48108

Cover art by Leah Myers

Interior design Kathy Campbell

ISBN 978-0-9767932-4-3

# CONTENTS

## PART 4
### Tools for Reverent Engagement • 65

## PART 5
### What Happens When Women Play • 105

# REVERENT ENGAGEMENT

AS I SIT in my sacred writing spot watching the Canada geese graze and nap by the edge of the pond, I plug into their energy field. I have the fleeting thought, "*you can be my audience.*" Although it sounded like a funny thought at first, I immediately received another, "My writing and all of my work is in the service of beautiful Mother Earth and all of her creatures." So, in fact, I am writing for them.

What a surprising opening into the topic of "reverent engagement," a term coined by my dear friend, Victoria Hanchin, author of *The Seer and the Sayer: Revelations of the New Earth.*

Her book is a breathtaking chronicle of experiences created through reverent engagement over the course of two years with indigenous grandmother, Dona, of the Mohawk tribe at a sacred site called Serpent Mound in Ohio. Victoria kept me abreast of her experiences throughout the actual experiencing and the writing of her book. I had an eyewitness account of the magic created through reverent engagement.

In keeping with my intention that the geese be my audience and deepening my connection with the geese as I wrote, I become more aware of their world. As I watched about two dozen geese grazing, I noticed they were flanked at both ends of their group by two more standing guard. Closer to me were two smaller groups napping. Those groups, as well, had a sentinel protecting them from intruders as they slept.

Reverent engagement is a communication with the natural world that creates an awareness of messages sent by nature. Most of us know a little bit about how this was a way of life in indigenous cultures.

As I wrote I sneezed, which brought an abrupt end to the napping and grazing of the geese. I wondered, "*what is the message?*" What seemed to me to be such a small disturbance created a complete disruption. In my listening internally for the message, I heard, *The sentinels stand guard over those who are made vulnerable by their inattention in grazing and napping.*

How do we stand guard and protect that which is vulnerable—our Earth, defenseless animals, children, and those living in poverty? Where are the guardians of the vulnerable? An important question. Predators exist, but how are the most vulnerable protected? The geese have their own system. Where is the system within humanity? It certainly could be the laws, but the laws have been adjusted to protect the predators and not the vulnerable.

The other observation was that my one little sneeze disrupted everything. It seemed so small, yet the impact was enormous. Everything changed. We impact our natural environment in an almost infinite variety of ways every day, but we ignore the impact of our actions. I remembered the stories I heard as a child that Native Americans knew how to walk in the woods without disturbing a twig. We, on the other hand, roar through with bulldozers and gigantic drills rupturing Mother Earth, releasing toxic fluids into our ground-water, and exploding the ground, creating earthquakes.

What a powerful lesson the geese offered this afternoon, using reverent engagement. I thank them for their message.

As I reflected on the urgent need for guardians for Mother Earth, my friend Robin Milam pops into my mind. Robin is co-founder of an organization creating a Bill of Rights for Mother Earth. Clare Dubois who founded Tree Sisters is another powerful woman acting to protect Gaia. These two women act as guardians. Countless others invest their passion, time and energies in this way.

I was ending my experience of reverent engagement when a ladybug crashed into my head and landed on the paper I was writing on. Following the teachings of my friend Victoria I asked myself, *What is the message?* The old childhood verse popped into my mind: *Ladybug, ladybug, fly away home. Your house is on fire and your children will burn.* I wrote in *Sacred Marching Orders*, "The house is on fire and here is the water to put it out."

I believe the water to put it out is our own reverent engagement: with ourselves, with one another and with Mother Earth. As we listen and receive the messages, we act from love on behalf of all life. Living life with reverent engagement, immersed in deep listening, and then acting, motivated by love, is exactly what the world needs now.

# 3 TYPES OF REVERENT ENGAGEMENT

AS CHARLON, my editor, and I moved toward the completion of this book, it was clear to me that we were showing examples of three different types of reverent engagement.

The first type shows the experience of reverent engagement with Mother Earth—Part 2 of this book.

The second type is the reverent engagement I offered to each woman I interviewed through essence-to-essence communication, which yielded powerful wisdom and truth.

The third example was modeled by Charlon in her powerful tuning in and listening to her Inner Self as she sculpted each conversation.

In her role as editor she wielded magic as she unveiled masterpieces of each interview. The story of Michelangelo describing his creation of David as chipping away pieces of marble to reveal the statue of David was similar to the process I witnessed Charlon doing with each amazing offering of these 11 women.

Charlon shares: "As we diligently chip away at what is not us, what is underlying is the rarified version of our True Selves. Truly, we are masterpieces under the thick, dense stratum, laid one protective layer at-a-time due to trauma and conditioning, often in childhood.

"I wear the (invisible) gold star on my forehead. Mission accomplished. I can speak with authority about chipping at protective, insulating layers because I've done it.

"While I didn't have a language for it then, what I know now thanks to Patricia Fero, is that I was reverently-engaged in the process of *my own* becoming. (Because service to others and Mother Earth anchors when we have securely anchored our own inner landscape of Self.) I was determined to focus my efforts—figurative hammer and chisel in hand—until there was nothing left but my most potent Self. And yes, this investment has unearthed a masterpiece. While there may still be fine-tuning ahead, the great work is complete.

"This initiation equipped me to show up in ways that continue to delight and surprise me. My personal path of reverent engagement has illuminated my gift to humanity. And we all have at least one.

"While I have always revered the power of words to either nourish or destroy, through this transformative process I have discovered that my Divine Vocation is *energetic wordsmith.*

"My artistic medium is words. Yet, as I word-craft in the role of ghostwriter or editor, most importantly, it is mine to wield a softened gaze so I can view beyond the obvious and extract the purest essence and potential of written language. I am in service to the spirit of words. They inform me. Through reverent engagement, my being hears what they want to express and want to become. It is my job to be the vigilant human conduit for that to occur. And it always does. With consistently-astounding results.

Based on my innerstanding, this is the natural outcome of one's willingness to simply follow and enact Spirit's informed flow, revealed moment-to-moment.

"In this role as energetic wordsmith, I follow the pulse and act accordingly to dismantle, distill, infuse, layer, reconfigure, restore, sequence, uplevel, and whole, the energetic configurations and frequencies of the individual words, as well as the word-strings, to convey the message in its most potent form.

"In many ways, this function is a covert op. Similar to secret messages painted into the world's most famous paintings, this is the energetic version. Words contain energetic markers, aka characteristic energetic signatures. If the energies of even seemingly high-frequency words are heavy, dense, have jagged energetic edges, or are chaotic or incongruent with the intended message—which is how I experience them—that, there, is my work.

"I have no cognitive awareness of how or when, exactly, this is happening throughout the creative process. I do know that my human Self is immersed so deeply, does this work in other dimensions or is otherwise appropriated by Spirit that She loses substantial blocks of time. As one aspect of my human Self is occupied with writing and editing tasks that are (or seem to be) more structured—yet I hold a soft focus even here—simultaneously I am subtly aware of something magickal taking place that does not originate from my skill set, ego, mind, personality, or personal agenda. I experience it as a complimentary, dynamic companion energy to my human Self sat at a computer, fingers clacking at a keyboard.

"And while I might not know the *how* or *when*, the *why* does intrigue me. My best guess is that the thinking human has to be "out of the way," (aka in an altered state) for there to be a clear pathway for words to shape themselves according to a system that's not accessible to the ego/mind/personal agenda. Words have an inherent guiding wisdom for someone who can hear their frequency and unquestioningly places themselves in service to it. Clearly, I am that. I don't want results I—ego, mind, personality—could create. I want to experience the magick of a dynamic synergism between heaven and Earth/Divinity and humanity. And the only way I know to do that is to willingly surrender into setting Me aside. I do! In wholehearted reverent and entranced engagement, I do my part. The rest is in the hands of the Divine.

"In the blessed spirit of reverent engagement for the elevation of Mother Earth and humanity, it has been an honor that my hand and heart played a role in shaping this book. Ultimately, because you, dear reader, hold *this book* in *your hands*, it has been in service *to you*. Blessed Be."

*A river of birds in migration*
*A nation of women with wings*

—LIBANA

## PART 1

# WHAT HAPPENS WHEN WOMEN
# *Converge*

## 1

S EVERAL YEARS AGO I came across the phrase "A nation of women." I didn't remember where I saw it or heard it, but those words were so compelling to me that I wrote it in my daily planner and transferred those words year after year each time I began a new calendar in January. This may have happened for as many as 10 years.

In 2009 when I was attending a workshop of Gather The Women, I asked in circle if anyone was familiar with the phrase "A nation of women." One of the elder women in the group said it came from an old women's round with the verses, "A river of birds in migration, A nation of women with wings."

For many years I have seen my purpose as "igniting the role of the collective feminine in planetary awakening. As I have lived this role and observed the exponential expansion of women waking up in the last decade I came to an awareness of something like a click into the collective feminine like a convergence or confluence of women working in unison in the service of Mother Earth and all her inhabitants. Images of a murmuring of starlings that swoop and move as one kept coming to me as a "river of birds."

Grandmother Flor de Mayo of the 13 indigenous grandmothers divulged that the final glyph of the Mayan calendar which ended in 2012 showed the staff of power being handed to the feminine. I believe we have all witnessed a rising up of the feminine from hearing the term *waking up* and the word *woke* used in political lexicon.

My sense is that the mass awakening has now morphed into a nation of women as the song says, "A river of birds in migration, A nation of women with wings." This convergence or confluence can be seen and even experienced as the magical, mesmerizing image of a murmuring of starlings.

As most religions and spiritual beliefs lead us to our collective oneness in love, I see the rise and unification of the Divine Feminine providing the impetus and roadmap to this return to an experience of oneness and love.

The messages from Mother Earth in Part 2—and the qualities embodied by each of the 11 women featured in Parts 3 and 4—provide this roadmap.

As the collective feminine:

- We bestow our energies to the potential of the future.

- We dismantle ancestral codes of disconnection.

- We reclaim ancient powers of magic and love for global restructuring.

- We release the need to define our purpose.

- We remind each other to source power from the womb.

- We sanction our best efforts as enough.

- We amplify our yes by listening out and in.

- We create whole, harmonized, meditation practices.

- We wield rarified anger as the embodied energy of fiery passion.

- We weave a global web of connection with essence-to-essence conversation.

- We circle in action.

We converge, and we unearth the potency of the collective feminine through reverent engagement.

❖ PART 2 ❖

# REVERENT
# ENGAGEMENT
## WITH
## *Mother Earth*

## 2

# INTRODUCTION

O N MARCH 1ST, 2010, while meditating in my office I was amazed to find an impression of a face of a Native American man on the wall across from me.

I asked him his name and he told me, "White Pine." I had been channeling my sister Nene for several years, so it was natural for me to begin communicating with him.

The purpose of this content is to provide a tiny sampling of his words. He speaks with a clarity and urgency that I hope inspires you to action. His message is that we must move out of our denial and apathy.

Several years later I learned more about the appropriation of Native American spirituality and decided that I was being a part of that inappropriate use of First

Nations culture and stopped using the name White Pine for these writings.

I did, however, continue to trust the energy and wisdom that came when I sat in the woods and tuned into the voice of the natural world.

Unexpectedly, in one of my conversations I received the message, "I suggest you call this Messages from Mother." My internal conflict about wanting to be respectful of First Nations culture and knowing that I needed to continue to convey the message was solved.

The vibration, message and energy was the same and I became clear that what I called it was irrelevant. My dilemma was solved and my trust of my commitment to share the message was strengthened.

# The Messages

## The Fall

The Fall was a disconnection from our Mother Earth. It was a belief and an experience of separation. The return to heaven on earth is a return to the experience of oneness. That's what you've been experiencing most of today. It is not going to go away. The vibrational match to the natural world will continue now, and it will grow stronger.

# Return of the Indigenous

There was a time when people lived in harmony with nature. There was a time when people knew the sun was their father and the earth was their mother. There was a time when people knew the animals were their brothers and sisters and that nature was their home.

People have moved so far away from this truth in the past several thousand years. This New Earth is a return to that awareness. Every time you see a bird or an animal of any kind and you communicate with it with loving respect and attentive listening you are building an energetic bridge to the return of that way of life.

Knowing this is so important. You are co-creators with the Universe. People are responsible for what was lost and people are responsible for renewing what now lives in disarray. You are the only ones who can do this. What each of you do each time you do it matters because the universe is holographic. The revitalization of each tiny piece revitalizes the whole. I must repeat: what you do matters more than you are able to understand right now.

Communicate with everything and everyone with reverence, and the most powerful love you can engender. The New Earth will be ushered in by those of you who are willing and able to respond to this knowledge.

## We Are Wired to Connect

Listen to nature. You are wired to connect. Wired to listen. Listen, listen. If you would do this one thing—listen—there would be little that is more important.

## Becoming At Home In The Woods

Becoming at home in the woods means just that: becoming at home in the woods. It doesn't mean just walking through the woods for exercise and enjoying the scenery. It means sitting down, plugging in, and listening.

Reciprocal communication is most important because the natural world has so much wisdom for you and for these times. Also, being seen and appreciated is valuable for the natural world.

You just noticed how your heart opened up as you said these words and as you saw the crow in the distance. It expands your soul and connecting with your soul is crucial.

There is no better way to connect with your soul than to sit in the woods, plug in, and let the energy and the information flow through.

You are aware as we are doing this that the feeling deepens and expands the longer you stay here. Adopt this as a practice.

## Magic of the Natural World

Here you are, plugged in and ready to write. Notice how the birds and squirrels just became so much louder? You talk about a reciprocal communication with the natural world, but you don't really fully believe it yet.

The more you do it, the more you'll have these experiences. They're proof to you that this is Real. Trust the Reality of it. Deepen into the Magic of it.

Plugged in, tuned in, and listening. Now is the time for you to deepen your trust of this process. Not only is it real, but it is an extraordinarily powerful gift for humanity and for Mother Earth.

You have your assignment. You can call it Divine Assignment or Sacred Marching Orders. I suggest you call it *Messages from Mother*.

In so many religions people have been taught that they can speak to God and hear God. Why has it been so foreign to you to recognize that you can speak to this imminent spirit that is Mother Earth?

Since the beginning of the patriarchal age she has been defiled. This is her time of return.

She is speaking and many are listening. You are one of them. There are countless others. You all convey her voice and she has much to say. If Mother Earth and the natural world is not Magic, I don't know what is.

Those pictures you took this morning capture the essence of this Magic. Watching your dog Dexter romp through the high weeds led by his nose was breathtaking. What is Magic if it's not the beauty of the life force coursing through animals in total freedom, and flowers bursting open from the rich, moist soil?

Magic has been so maligned and defiled under patriarchy. More and more of you are consciously reconnecting with it. This precious planet is beauty without measure. There is a growing movement to restore her to her original state.

You humans can be a part of this restoration or she can return to her fullness and opulence sans human beings.

It's the most important movement that has existed since the beginning of time. Stay the course and keep moving. We are participating with you.

## More Magic

Today I'm going to talk to you more about Magic and what it is. Its aliveness. Its light. Its Darkness. Its Beauty. Its love. Its connection. Its Unity. Its color.

These are all aspects of Magic. No one talks about

Magic anymore. It was overridden by mechanics and lifelessness. Hierarchical dominion over the natural world and all humans who were not powerful white men was a paradigm that did its best to destroy Magic.

Magic is returning because it must and it can. Be a bringer of the magic. Immerse yourself in the magic. Live in the magic. Now go take your dog Dexter for his magical walk in the woods.

Your companion animals are a bridge between the Western material world—devoid of connection—with the magic of the real world.

Remember when that history teacher told you the Greek philosophers like Aristotle and Socrates used the word Real with an uppercase R to write or speak about the natural world of spirit? The lowercase *real* described man-made world devoid of spirit. Where you are now sitting on a moss covered fallen tree with Dexter romping and chewing on sticks is the Real world. You are learning that this Real world is communicating to you and your job is to listen and to hold this world in your heart.

The woodpecker is delivering her message for you now. She is pecking insistently giving you the message of persistence in hearing, scribing, and delivering my message.

Listen to the bird that is calling so loudly. It's a robin and it is a harbinger of spring. You're surprised that I'm using the word harbinger. I carry the White Pine energies of the name and identity that are presented to you, but I am so much more.

Feel the energy here. You can smell it and feel the green returning. In a month, this area will be covered with Trillium and Sweet William and bloodroots. We are making our way up to the light through the dark, moist, pregnant soil. We will burst forth in a show of brilliance just around the corner.

I use the word *corner* intentionally because I want to talk to you about the contrast between corners, and circles and Magic.

Magic was exiled from your world intentionally because Magic is the most powerful force in the universe.

Corners are man-made and linear. This energy had its time but it is now over. Enough of you are returning to the World of Magic. Magic has survived.

Remember the line from The Buffy Sainte-Marie song—God is alive. Magic is afoot. You are here, deeply immersed in it. It has always been here waiting. Love it. Love it and go on your way.

See how at home your dog Dexter feels? He loves

the leaves and the dirt and he explores and sniffs everything. He digs and chews sticks and frolics. He's at home here. Learning to become at home in the woods is a step forward that you non-indigenous can take. Become at home in the woods. Look for ways to do this.

This will help: tap in and notice how different it feels to know you are a part of this Magic. We are Magic, you know. Your people gave up Magic when the patriarchal system took over. The Magic has never gone away. You just stopped tapping into it.

## Hearing the Voice of Earth's Intelligence

Look at the beauty of everything alive. Do you think Mother Earth has an intelligence? How could it possibly be otherwise? You believe you have an intelligence, but so much of it is from your brain and things you have learned from outside yourself. A lot of that is like being a recorder. Information comes in and you retain it and then process it through the patterns and belief systems you've often created in the service of defending against your vulnerability. This is the way you learned to live.

If you believe everything alive has a voice, how do you learn to listen to all this intelligence? One crucial way is to get out of your head and into your body. You have the gift of being clairaudient. That means you can share messages from other dimensions without using the more traditional ways of hearing with your physical ears.

## Our Future Depends On Us Attuning to the Natural World

The focus on future denies the demise of the planet, humankind, and animals, and exclusively focuses on scientific accomplishments meant to create the future we desire. The future of life on Earth, and the quality of life here, is startlingly absent in conversations.

We see the future in terms of goals and accomplishments and see that as progress. We neglect the glaring reality of how close we are to following the path of extinction that thousands of species have suffered.

What if we brought into daily experience and conversations the gifts and guidance of our ancestors?

What if we made a daily choice to take a seat in the natural world and listen to the wisdom and guidance of Mother Earth?

What if we moved out of this despicably self-centered, comfortable perspective that we, and those like us, are the only ones that matter?

What if we experienced every day as a true day of

remembering all of our relations in this realm and others?

Tuning in, focusing, and listening is not such a difficult thing to do. It merely requires quiet, focus, and intention. The guidance is there for us. Let's step out of our familiar comfort zone and tap in. The lives of everything and everyone depend on it.

## Everything Wants To Offer Its Gifts

Listening within and listening without. The natural world is always speaking to you, but you don't take the time to listen.

Cell phones and iPods are so destructive. You spoke last night about how you are disconnected from one another as a result of communication through technology—Facebook, texting, cellphones.

There's another level that's even more significant that is so lost, you don't even think about it. That is communicating with nature. Everything that is alive wants to be seen and heard and offer its gifts. Just as you are in alignment with your Core Essence Self when you are offering your gifts, so does everything in the natural world want to offer its gifts.

So many gifts ignored, denied, unopened. So much beauty unseen, so much wisdom unheard. You have become such wasteful, ungrateful people. You ignore and lay waste to such magnificence. It's crucial that this stop and that this stop sooner, rather than later.

## Return To The Sacred Connection

When you see a bird put your attention on the bird. At the same time move your attention into your heart. Extend loving energy to the bird from your heart. Picture or imagine the energetic connection between you and the bird. Feel the energy flowing from the bird to your heart. Listen with your inner ear to the message the bird is delivering to you. Trust what is happening. Don't use your brain to discount, diminish, or deny what you are receiving.

Let's do more.

&#x26A6; **WATER.** Sit on the ground beside a body of water. Close your eyes and imagine yourself merging with the water. Water is fluid. To speak the language of water you must make yourself fluid. Imagine yourself filled with liquid and light. Allow your form to dissolve and experience yourself flowing into the body of water you're sitting beside. Feel the essence that is you floating on the body of water. Feel yourself as separate, but one within the larger body of water.

⚹ **ROCK.** Find a big, powerful rock to sit on. Feel the strength and power of the rock against your tailbone. Feel and picture the red energy of your root chakra moving down into the red core of Mother Earth. The stability and density of the rock assists you in connecting deeply and powerfully with the core of the Earth. Listen and feel.

These are powerful and practical exercises that create and strengthen the return to the sacred connection—soul-to-soul—of the natural world and all that is living.

## Seven Steps for Listening to Nature

1. Get out of your house and into a natural setting.

2. Remove electronic devices from your ears.

3. Move your attention out of your head, within your body, and into your heart.

4. Open your eyes and focus on the Real world around you.

5. Pay attention to the sounds and sights you behold.

6. Extend loving energy from your heart to all that you behold.

7. Hold it all within your heart with appreciation.

## Urgency

You talk about urgency but you do not act with urgency. You waste so much time. It's almost like you're doing it for entertainment. This is not about entertainment. This enlightenment is not a hobby. Engage. Act. Jump. This is jump time. You have to find a way to stay in the moment while I am speaking to you. It is a fine line to act with urgency without elevating fear. This is the focus of my work with you. Do not fear: act now.

You are right that I speak with a sense of urgency. Each atrocity, all violence that is perpetrated against the earth and any living thing is a disturbance to those of us who are fully alive, though not in human form. Passivity and patience are no longer acceptable. You lay waste to the bountiful, beautiful gifts of Earth—gifts in your stewardship. The pain is beyond description.

WAKE UP! STOP IT! These are the times of great opportunity, of great need. Pay attention to what is happening around you, happening to your earth and take action with all your heart and power. When you act with fierceness and love, you begin returning the gifts in your stewardship to all living things.

## PART 3

# Inspiration
## FOR
# REVERENT
# ENGAGEMENT

# 3

# WE BESTOW

(Phyllis Curott)

---

**We Bestow** Our Energies to the Potential of the Future
as inspired by a conversation with Phyllis Curott

---

THE WORD *witch*—which actually means *Wise One*—conjures forth negative fears of women's power, spirituality and sexuality that have been projected onto women throughout time. Owning and saying the word; reclaiming and redeeming the word, are tangible acts that confront the patriarchal culture and its historic mistreatment of women.

While lots of women are now using the term *witch* for precisely these reasons, the journey to get here has been one of great sacrifice. The leading edge of systemic change is often initiated by one person; an evolutionary whose role it is to challenge the status quo, create the container and protect the integrity of the container until a time when it can then be held by many hands.

The *World's Parliament of Religions* was inaugurated in Chicago in September, 1893. Celebrating 100 years in 1993 led to a new series of conferences under the official title *Parliament of the World's Religions*. While fresh themes were integrated into the new program, the modern version adhered to the original goal of creating an inclusive forum for a global dialogue of faiths.

In 1993, Phyllis Curott took the first steps in an effort to legitimize Wicca as a religion by attending The Parliament. Unaware of it at the time, that singular action would begin the ripple of concentric circles to activate core change worldwide for the benefit of women *and* men.

Early in Phyllis's involvement, a definitive shift was made that changed the course of The Parliament itself. The day and evening before Parliament formally opened, only men were on-stage. A woman rabbi was the emcee, but there were no women participants. The power imbalance was obvious. And from the back of the room literally came the cry. More than 4,000 women among the 8,000 attendees chanted, "Where are the women?" This had never happened before, and it was obvious, suddenly, how much of the energy of the Parliament was the gift of the women who had been participating, supporting and helping this organization over the years as volunteers, donors and attendees.

When their absence in leadership became conspicuous, they were empowered to say something, which resonated throughout Parliament. Giving a voice sets change in motion. Back it with action and the momentum cannot be stopped.

Attending Parliament every year except one since the 100th anniversary, as each year passed, Phyllis's passion, involvement, and responsibilities increased. A public Wiccan Priestess from 1982, it's not in her nature to be stereotyped or pigeonholed in negative ways; e.g. "I will not wear green-face." And as a feminist and activist practicing the rebirth of this ancient faith tradition—which always honored the divine feminine and not just masculine, and had a role for women as priestesses and spiritual leaders—she brings deep reverence for its origins and rituals. True to her beliefs and mission, she knew this must continue in any involvement with The Parliament.

Later, Phyllis would be the first Wiccan priestess to be invited to sit on the Board of Trustees, which was a thrill and honor. Serving previously on the Harvard University Pluralism Project for diversity in American faith traditions, Phyllis had been active in the interfaith community in New York. If not for her background as an Ivy League-schooled lawyer, equipped with a keen track record and widespread honoring in the work she'd done as a very public Wiccan priestess, she might not have been included so readily. Yet there she was, facing one of life's great opportunities to shift the current status quo in a big way; from the inside.

By 2015, Phyllis knew there had to be a women's plenary, a women's assembly, and women's programming for the annual Parliament. In her role as Board Member, she advocated for it and with focused effort, it happened.

She used her legal skills to analyze the bylaws and created a strategy for compliance. The assembly was hosted outside of the Parliament, as an event that preceded the Parliament in order to maintain autonomy with the programming. For the first time, concurrent to Parliament itself, scheduled programming featured women speakers on womens' issues. In addition, a sacred space—the Red Tent—was created for women, and a gender-specific plenary was attended by more than 1,000 women.

Women have always been told to sit down and wait their turn. It seems there's always something else to resolve before womens' rights are addressed. The Civil Rights movement comes first. Ending the war comes first. The environmental collapse comes first. And women are told, always, even now, that their self-defined safety and rights are secondary. And women have taken that in as a patriarchal introject, as well. We internalize it.

For Phyllis, it came down to a singular moment in answering a Divine call. She illuminates, "I just was like, nope, this is the moment. I'm the person. I'm the one here. It's on me. I'm going to do it. And it was incredible. I didn't know what impact it would have. I still don't fully know. All that effort, all the hard work really meant something to me personally, no doubt about it. It was the measure of my moral courage to do the right thing."

Sisters, we've waited long enough. Now, we will neither be stopped nor stifled.

Using the platforms created for women concurrent to Parliamentary programming, women spoke candidly and in great detail. Yet, their energy was gorgeous, gracious and joyous. They embodied all the positive aspects of their individual faith traditions. Gratitude was prominent.

When given the opportunity, they expressed their grievances with grace and dignity. What was clear is that they want access to full participation, whatever the religion. And it's to the honoring of that pure message that keeps the movement of inclusion growing.

The beautiful irony is that by giving space for universal expression and representation, it makes institutions more vital, more engaged, more alive, fuller, more realized. If women are cut out, essentially half of the truth of every faith is excised. Every time faith diminishes women, it cuts them off and contradicts the essential tenets of its own spiritual truth and it becomes politics; sexual politics. Faith contradicts itself when it demeans, denies or suppresses women.

When women ally, they support each other. Not only in the expression of what's wrong, but in the uplifting of what's right. And it makes their lives richer. It makes sisterhood stronger. It affirms the pain they've suffered, but also the possibility of that pain being healed and transformed.

Moving forward, the Parliament shines as a beacon

for open-hearted progressive willingness to speak about things that don't have an opportunity to be addressed elsewhere. The most important thing now is that women have the stage. What they choose to say is up to them.

> What's important to women? What have they experienced? What lives in their hearts? What motivates them? What drives them? What wisdom do they possess? What gifts they are willing to offer? What are they willing to share with each other? What impact are they having on the world?

In a glance backward, Phyllis clearly sees what her initiative inspired in other women and other organizations, but admits it wasn't easy. That's often what it's like to be a revolutionary. You're surrounded by those who want to talk about the minutia instead of divvying up the workload, making decisions, and getting to the hard work. Others may not "get it," be engaged, captivated or motivated by the big vision. It may not resonate or be compelling enough to elicit action. Yet, you know your purpose within this seemingly-impossible mission and you get to it with eyes and heart faced forward.

The adage is: If you build it, they will come. But building happens single-brick-by-single-brick. Time passes and in those quiet, late-night moments it's natural to wonder: will all this effort make any difference now or in the future? The truth is: you may not know the impact that you're having. Ever. Yet, you give it your all because that's the invitation showing up.

Going in, you may wonder if you have the character and courage; the stamina and strength. Throughout the process you may be fully tested, especially when standing alone, for what you think is important. You may go in revved-up and emerge exhausted, but you'll respect yourself.

So, one never knows if what they're doing will make a difference, but we can surrender that wondering because ultimately, it's not about us. Our actions are our greatest offering to the potential of the future. We make our unique contributions whole heartedly with the knowledge that the rest is not up to us. Forces much larger than the individual take it from there. Ultimately, your actions are the gifts given to yourself, womanhood, humanity and the planet.

Phyllis is living proof that one person can make a difference that reaches around the world. A series of singular, strategically implemented, seemingly insignificant individual actions at a time, created the platform for sanctioned, unfiltered expression for women. These many focused efforts opened doors, created opportunities, and broke glass ceilings.

Now these presentations, platforms, and programs are much more mainstream, but that's what happens, right? Change is an evolutionary process. In the beginning, a huge investment of resources is required to set the movement into action including time, energy, focus, money and expertise. And when critical mass is reached, change expresses widely as its fresh, new form.

About the last 40 years Phyllis says, "I felt that my job was to create the container and protect the integrity of the container until the seeds sprouted. And that then, within that sacred space; within that holy grail; within that womb, women would make their own magic. They would make their own connections; they would express what they needed to; they would generate the Divine expressions they had waited so long to share."

She positioned herself to advance womens' inclusion by fighting for what she believed to be right and the true measure of the Parliament itself: its openness, its willingness to embrace the other and to give the other an honored position to speak from their heart, even if it was uncomfortable. She had to. It was her contribution to make. And if she was going to do it at all, she was determined to take it all the way.

# 4

# WE DISMANTLE

## (Leah Myers)

---

**We Dismantle** Ancestral Codes of Disconnection
as inspired by a conversation with Leah Myers

---

ACH OF US has experienced it: we set an intent and on the heels of that focus, our own version of resistance materializes. While it was lying there all along, there's something about setting intent or moving in an unfamiliar direction that immediately brings hesitation, self-doubt, and negative mind talk to the forefront. And then we are at a choice point. Do we choose to back away, setting a new path aside yet again, or do we honor, value and examine that resistance with curiosity to see what more there is to know about moving beyond it?

Through external influences, we've been pro-grammed from the moment of conception. Religious, educational and familial institutions make their insidi-ous marks to shape us according to accepted norms. And woven into these programs are disconnection codes. (Resistance is only one example.)

Most disconnection codes run on autopilot, just under the level of our awareness so we don't question them. But when we begin to notice, there are threads of disconnection interwoven in the way we think, speak and act.

Much of what we discover when exploring dis-connection codes is that they are in place to protect us from connecting. And it's time to dismantle them because we don't need them anymore. What's being called forth now to move us forward into New Earth living is real, authentic, vulnerable connection. Fortu-nately, that is made easier by discerning the difference between connection codes and disconnection codes.

## Identifying the Codes Through Feeling

There is a numbness to disconnection codes. You cannot feel anything deeply. You feel separated from what's going on. You're not able to engage fully. Aspects of you might be engaged, but you're unable to be fully present. The busy ego mind occupies this space and tries to provide insight or move toward understanding by intellectualizing (which never works anyway!). Disconnection codes are characterized as life-diminishing.

But when you're running a connection code, you're fully engaged, you're fully present, you're not in your head, your heart is open, and you feel the intensity of everything in the best way. You feel vibration throughout your body. You feel even the subtlest incoming messages and energies. Connection codes are characterized as life affirming.

Moving into the new paradigm is all about consciously and deliberately shifting onto the next higher turns of the spiral. Related to dis/connection, this leap we take occurs as we become aware of disconnection codes and shift them to connection in the moment, every time they surface. It's the action following awareness that has so much power. And this action is the springboard for launching us into the new paradigm.

## Leah's Connection Story

"The best way to make this relatable is to just share my own experience.

"It showed up for me when I set a simple intention to paint more. While I've always felt very drawn to painting and it's a place that my soul wants to go, for whatever reason, I faced resistance. I wanted to shift or heal whatever that was, so I made an intention to start painting. And I followed it up by connecting with another friend who also wanted to paint more. To hold each other accountable, we committed to meeting every Monday and devote at least an hour to painting. We also aimed to talk about the experience and share what showed up that we wanted to work through.

"What she and I assumed would be a joyful, fun space actually launched a huge episode of healing. And what I came to realize is that it was specifically healing to examine the disconnection programming that runs through me.

"When you paint, you are in full connection. You are connecting to your soul, you're connecting to yourself, you're connecting to your environment, you're wiring everything up.

"When I went into the space to paint, I consistently hit a wall of resistance that I felt, but had no awareness around. I didn't know exactly what it was, why it was showing up, or how to move through it. Setting the intention to increase my awareness brought in a series of healers in different modalities that helped me work with the energy as it was showing up.

"The first healer I met was a meditation coach. She helped open a space for me to hear myself. That brought in a wave of healing. From there, I worked with another healer who facilitated deep, intensive meditations. One of them—a sacred womb healing—sent golden light energy through my ancestral lines to clear emotional baggage. And in working with a body healer, long-forgotten memories came into my consciousness. Through these different modalities and healers, I started to get a comprehensive picture of my invisible wall of resistance.

"What showed up was disconnection codes running through my DNA—my ancestral lines. And the purpose of these codes was to point me in the direction of discovering more of my history and that of my ancestors. Naturally, that led to genealogical research. One next-opening always leads to another.

"During this time of healing, something interesting showed up: as an image in my head, several male ancestors were standing, one behind the other, holding vigil. I call them sentinels. They were silently holding a protective, guarded stance.

"What I came to understand is that the wall of resistance I was hitting within myself was this line of male ancestors. When I dug further into the history, I found out that going backward in time from the American Revolutionary War of the late 1700's, there were generations of military history—male ancestors who had been in one war after another. I came to understand that their codes of survival were the codes of disconnection. And it made perfect sense!

"One cannot survive being on the battlefield without being disconnected. When you're connected, you feel every pain in your body and all the emotional pain around you. For them to survive thousands of years of domination, in war and in battle, they would have to enact codes of survival including disconnection.

"Those disconnection codes served a purpose and kept them alive. In that way, these codes were invaluable. And they passed on these very same codes to me. They run through me. I can feel them. But they've outlived their purpose and it's time for me to shift them to the contrasting polarity: connection. And I couldn't do that without understanding the full story.

"Without understanding exactly what was running through me, and why, witnessing who my ancestors were, and being with their pain was essential to my discovery of these disconnection codes and in moving through my personal process. I came into understanding through these moments when I was connecting with them, their pain, the deep pain of disconnection, and how they've held so much suffering in their bodies. I had to hold how painful and courageous that was for them. They didn't have a choice. But they were able to keep the genetics alive through running these codes.

"When I felt them fully and witnessed their pain that was held in *my* own being, and allowed it to move through me while I showed honor, respect and value for it, it created an opening to have a conversation with them. I said, "I honor and value your codes of disconnection and everything you've given me. I'm standing on your shoulders and I'm so grateful. But in order for me and humanity to survive now, we have to shift out of disconnection. If we keep running the codes of disconnection, we're not going to survive.

"Human needs are completely different now. We have to connect. We have to connect to our souls. We have to connect to our feelings. We have to connect to our emotions. We have to connect to our bodies. We have to feel everything. That's what's needed. We have to allow our feelings and value our feelings because that's what's informing what needs to shift, change and heal, so we create a future where we thrive.

"Our safety and security was in disconnection, but that's no longer true. Our safety and security is now in connection. We have to know that at first it feels vulnerable, awkward and uncomfortable. But if we keep up this dialogue, and explore healing with our ancestors, we can make this essential shift."

# 5

# WE RECLAIM

(Katherine Schaaf)

---

**We Reclaim** Ancient Powers of Magic
and Love for Global Restructuring
as inspired by a conversation with Katherine Schaaf

---

W E ARE LIVING in unprecedented times of breakdown. (In the United States) our entire democracy has already broken down. A system of checks and balances that we thought was in place isn't working as it once did. And that is just one aspect. Add climate crisis, and the enormity of the resulting earth changes that are only going to intensify, and it's obvious: we are in deep shit.

This enormous, catastrophic shift that's happening on a planetary scale is a reflection of a systemic disease. And outdated ways can't begin to address this system-wide breakdown. Doing things in the old way isn't enough. Our mission now is to explore what many would describe as "new technologies." Actually, they are ancient technologies; the age old practices of alchemy, transmutation and magic.

In his book *The Magdalene Manuscript*, Tom Kenyon channeled Mary Magdalene, who described how she was trained in alchemy and magic in Egypt. In turn, she taught them to Christ. That's how he was able to resurrect. This isn't new. Magic isn't a new thing. It's an ancient thing that we need to rediscover and reclaim as our own to shift our global direction. And women will lead the charge.

Women used to be trained in alchemy; in the formulas; in ritualistic practices and ceremony. In many ways in recent years, we have borrowed the ceremonial ritual sacred practices of the indigenous people because that was all we had access to. Yet borrowing is not the same as embodying and knowing for ourselves.

In addition to remembering and implementing the arts of alchemy, transmutation and magic, we need to reconnect with our own ancestral lineage of spiritual practice, ceremony, ritual… whatever word you want to use. Each of us has something unique to bring. And it's imperative to make the distinction about the rights and rituals of others and our own. Ownership through embodiment is what will shift us into lasting change.

While you may hear and appreciate the drum beat of another, that beat may be out of sync with the knowing of your own ancestry. We are each pulsing on our unique frequency spectrum.

At least initially, restoring ancient systems to our planet isn't a matter of reclaiming a singular, global beat, for there are many threads to a single tapestry. It's about becoming aware of your own beat. When you come into that full sensory awareness, you'll be able to quickly, accurately and neutrally assess that these other drumbeats are not of *your* ancestors. When you experience the pounding on the skin drum accompanied by the singing of an ancient song and it's yours, it's unmistakable. Your body confirms it. The hairs on your body stand at attention, signaling an ancient clarion call. A part of you remembers your unique spiritual lineage, which is distinct from that of other cultures.

The deep dives we've explored in recent years is the

invitation for all women, regardless of where they're from. We all need to reconnect with that somehow and discover for ourselves our own drum beat, our own songs, our own sound. And then we bring that to sacred circle with other women where the cohesion of all beats occur; beaming outward as a single, harmonious, unified sound.

It's in that container, or cauldron, where we create enough safety and over time, an intimacy, that we can truly be ourselves. It's in the sacredness of circle that we know we will be held, heard, respected, and loved. And that doesn't happen the first time a circle gathers. It comes with devotion and repetition. It's at the third, fourth, eighth or 12th gathering in circle when a tipping point is reached; where there is enough safety and trust to birth something really big through the power of love.

A video clip of two Popes reveals something potent: Pope Francis, the incoming pope, is talking to Pope Benedict, the outgoing law and order Pope. Pope Francis says, "The truth may be vital. But without love, it is unbearable." And that feels so powerful today. We are being faced with so many truths that are unbearable, yet somehow we know love is the magic.

And it doesn't just involve love for others... it begins

with self-love. For women that is very challenging. We find it so much easier to tend to others, to care for others, to love others and to put them first. We find it much more difficult to love and nurture ourselves. The reason, in part, is a result of patriarchy; those subtle and not-so-subtle messages about the feminine.

The other reason it's a challenge to love ourselves is that women across the planet carry geographic trauma in their DNA. As an example, women of European descent still carry cellular memory of The Burning Times. The trauma was so intense and profound that to this day it prevents us from stepping fully into our power. There is a deeply embedded fear of being seen and being known. To our cellular systems, either is dangerous, so we hold back, to the detriment of all.

In 2016, Pat McCabe began having vivid visions and dreams of The Burning Times; the pyre, torture, beatings, etc. Because the experiences were increasingly traumatizing—she was afraid to sleep at night—she asked a shaman for help. He told her that they would only stop when she took a group of Indigenous women from around the world back to Europe to do ceremony on that land. They were to heal the wound of the feminine.

She gathered women from diverse indigenous traditions, including Asian, African, North American, and South American. When she later wrote about the trauma, she said, "*It was designed to kill our soul as women.*" And the energy of that wound is still alive in the hearts of so many women. Most have absolutely no idea how insidious it is; how it expresses through our thoughts, words and actions.

It doesn't even occur to us to ask ourselves: *Where's the source of this self-doubt? What is the source of this fear of being seen, of showing up, of standing in my power?* We don't realize how deeply unconscious it is and that it's been transmitted multi-generationally for hundreds of years.

How can we shift these influences and ultimately, shift the current course?

Commissioned to take a leadership role in change, it is now ours to access and wield *all* the tools in our tool kit.

We have been equipped with ancient knowledge. Just as we carry trauma from the past in our DNA, so do we carry the wisdom. Let's use it in every way imaginable and innovative, according to our unique calling.

Love is a mighty force. We can learn to love ourselves. And then we can come into circle with others to experience fully being ourselves; to take ownership and be the leaders we're here to be. We can finally stop playing small and pretending that we don't know what we know. These behaviors effect so many women and they stand between us remembering how to do magic, but most importantly, that *we are magic.*

As women, we are here to harness the powers of magic and love to accomplish what some might call "impossible," yet we know better.

# 6

# WE RELEASE

(Rose Tenaglia Dunn)

---

**We Release** the Need To Define Our Purpose
as inspired by a conversation with Rose Tenaglia Dunn

---

WE COME INTO the world securely tethered to the knowing of Self by a golden thread. Over time we're conditioned to relinquish our self trust and adapt to the disconnected and distorted norms of culture, which are permeated by groupthink.

Over the past few years, the buzz about discovering one's life purpose has infiltrated and dominated spiritual circles. It's now hit the mainstream. It seems everyone wants access to what's on the other side of knowing the larger reason for being here. The premise is that once we are aware of our life purpose, we can rest into it and give ourselves permission to finally breathe again. And maybe create happier lives. *All will be well*, we think, *if only we know our purpose.*

The pressure to identify our purpose is immense. Knowing is portrayed by others as a holy, nirvanic panacea; the end-all, be-all. Countless books, online resources, and New Earth leaders emphasize the importance of knowing the role(s) we play in serving humanity and/or the planet. Our individual and collective future depends on it, or at least it feels that way.

It dominates our attention. We jump into the fray of action toward knowing our purpose without slowing down long enough to question what we're doing and why. The impulse is so tantalizing we simply follow the masses. But to what end? And to what detriment in the process?

Compressed by internal or external influences, it may even seem like a fierce competition. Disappointment and envy surge when we see that others have "found theirs," while in our own (mis)perception, we lag behind. *What's wrong with me?* may cross our minds. Instead of it being a play-infused, childlike process of delightful discovery, knowing our purpose has become yet one more arduous task to complete on the spiritual path.

When we peek beyond the obvious to reveal what's truly underlying this push, however, we see so clearly. Aha! It's the latest, faddish, shiny object; another charged pursuit fueled by an agenda; one more in a series of seemingly never ending dangling carrots toward enlightenment; a colossal distraction from living fully in every "this" moment.

(This isn't to say that knowing our purpose isn't helpful or informative. However, it's our approach that ultimately makes all the difference in our experience of it.)

We live in a world where we are taught all the answers are outside us. That's not true. The answers are within, where for myriad reasons, so many of us fail to look.

This tale makes the point:

> The Universe asked, "Where shall I hide the answers to life?" Came the response from the ethers, "You could hide it at the bottom of the ocean." To that the Universe replied, "I won't hide it at the bottom of the ocean because man will eventually get there. Another entity added, "How about hiding it in the heavens?" "Man will get there, too," answered the Universe. Coming to its own conclusion, the Universe said, "I know where I'll hide it… inside of man. He'll never look there."

Instead of trying to find your purpose with an outward focus or an external push, go within. Everything you'll ever need to understand about the meaning of life—and so much more—is found there, the seeds planted by the Creator.

Beyond knowing our purpose, how do we reinvigorate that Golden tether we were born with (by Divine plan, it could never be completely severed), strengthen our self-trust and gently lean into why we are here (if that is an essential element to our individual path)?

The process begins by getting really quiet. Quieting the mind, listening to the Divine within, trusting that inner voice, and channeling it into tangible action is a sacred practice. At first it may require a great deal of uncoiling old thought and behavioral patterning. That takes time and practical implementation. With a few rounds, the process becomes easier.

And by then, you might be surprised to realize that the urgency to know your mission diminishes. It no longer matters the way it did before. Knowing is a function of the mind that appeals to the ego. Not needing to know is a function of the heart that trusts all is well regardless of knowing our purpose.

Each of us experiences learning to trust the inner

voice in our own way. Our programming is so deeply embedded that we think we think we're insane when we start hearing these messages. It's a natural part of the process to wonder, *Is this even real? Am I losing my mind? How can I trust this?*

When we get to the point where we really trust these messages, we gain the confidence to take appropriate action without question or hesitation. The more you practice, the more you trust. The more you trust, the more opportunities you'll have to practice. Refinement happens as a direct result of your dedication to the process.

You might wonder how to decipher between your ego/mind and your inner voice when messages come to you. The voice of your inner wisdom delivers messages while you're in a relaxed state, and often while you're doing something unrelated to what you're thinking about.

However you strengthen the tether to your pure-Self and The Divine, your connection is one of a kind. It is exclusively yours to experience and explore. Make it right *with* you and it will be right *for* you. Find your own way to slow down, go within, stay within, listen, hear, trust, and enact the messages that come through.

Maybe we don't trust this methodology because it seems so simplistic; too simple to work; too contrasting to cultural indoctrination to lead us anywhere we'd really want to go.

We have been conditioned to look to the external for confirmations, solutions, or next steps toward realizing our life mission. We focus our efforts in the outer world, when if there is any work to be done, it is to go within.

Taking a deeper look into why a benevolent force would have hidden the answers to life inside us—other than because we are not inclined to look there—maybe, just maybe, it was for the pure pleasure of bread-crumbing us into discovering meaning within *for ourselves*. After all, we never forget those experiences that are our own discoveries. When we look within, we find wisdom within which eclipses the need to define our purpose and we are then free to live beyond that narrow pursuit.

# WE REMIND

(Elizabeth Wangler)

---

**We Remind** Each Other To Source Power From The Womb
as inspired by a conversation with Elizabeth Wangler

---

THERE IS A direct correlation between bears hibernating and women retreating into sacred space. Just as a bear crawls into a cave to hibernate for the winter, women know when to retreat into the energetic womb for restoration, transformation, inspiration and illumination.

Some returns are more passive, prompted by exhaustion, fatigue or uncertainty. Our reserves depleted, we surrender into retreat, like leaning way back in a comfortable chair knowing we'll be fully supported.

It's there we can truly rest. And in that moment, our higher self knows we need to slow to a stop. The womb becomes the haven where we slough off what was and allow the organic process of transformation to have its way with us as we slumber. It contains its own wisdom that realigns and reorients us for our next turn of The Wheel. And we trust its transformation process, often because we have no energies to resist.

Other returns to the warm, womb cocoon are comprised of eagerness and anticipation... when we are curious, energized and ready for our next quantum leap. We feel *something*, but may not know exactly what wants to be birthed. We lean in to listen deeply and await an infusion of specific information and inspiration that propels us forward.

Whether by leaning back or leaning in, we are led into this potent sanctum by a subtle felt-sense, an inner knowing, or a Divine directive that is undeniable. We may retreat for a few minutes—or even a few years— into the Source within. When the process is complete and we emerge from the silence, we then see our next steps through refocused eyes. The path ahead is clear. And we are equipped to wield new powers toward realizing the next expanded version of ourselves.

There's an intricately intertwined relationship between women and The Womb. After eons of separation through patriarchal attempts to completely sever the connection, we are just now returning to explore its mysteries and inherent healing powers. And it seems our planetary future depends on us harnessing the gifts of the womb, now.

You see, wombs—physical, energetic or both—are the carriers of life. And as women we are now called into action to enliven humanity, the Earth and all creation. It is our time to anchor an unprecedented reconnection with the natural world—to every single thing in creation both animate and inanimate—by first returning to our own sacred womb space whenever the call beckons. When we rest, restore and create from the Sacred Source within, we subtly yet potently rebuild the harmonious interdependent systems essential to our future.

As we go about the business of our everyday lives, it's important to remember to return to our personal inner sanctum that holds the ancient wisdom applicable to modern times. The energetic pattern held by this practice naturally illuminates the way for others. Our actions remind other women to source from within for themselves, which amplifies the benefit for all life. One by one, we create New Earth with our actions.

Whether we enter the portal of the vesica pisces toward the womb's wisdom for deep healing or to spark creation, it is there we consistently discover the resources only the womb can provide.

# 8

# WE SANCTION

(Linda Bender)

---

**We Sanction** Our Best Efforts As "Enough"
as inspired by a conversation with Linda Bender

---

THE GLOBAL NEED to champion Mother Earth, and all life upon Her, is especially evident right now. An undeniable quickening is happening. It's as if Her life, and ours, depends on our actions. It's searingly obvious to those with hearts to hear, see and feel.

This is the moment to respond to Her invitation to rise up, unite, and enact in every way possible based on our unique gifts, interests and ordained contributions. Even so, at times this call to action can be overwhelming to the individual who wonders if one person really can make a difference.

Whether we identify as activists or not, it is so easy to go crazy and feel that whatever we are doing is just not enough. You may think, *Oh my god, it's overwhelming. I feel like giving up because the vast need eclipses my singular contribution.*

For Linda, this shows up related to helping animals. She holds a doctorate degree in veterinary medicine and is a lifelong animal advocate. During the fourteen years she lived in Europe, Asia, Africa, and the Middle East, her work included the rescue, rehabilitation, and protection of wildlife. Linda delivers workshops and lectures worldwide on the relationship between humans, animals and nature.

In times of private contemplation, she thinks of the quiet strength required to simply carry on. Ultimately, she knows that whatever is going on in the world—in her personal life, in her professional life, related to the environment, and within government—each of us has total control of how we respond with our words, thoughts, actions and interactions.

Linda often sources the life of Viktor Frankl as her inspiration to remain motivated when she wonders if what she's doing has true meaning in the world and will translate as lasting change.

Born in 1905, Viktor Frankl was an Austrian neurologist and psychiatrist, and a Holocaust survivor. He was the founder of logotherapy—literally "healing through meaning"—and author of over 39 books. Most notably of these is his best-selling Man's Search for Meaning based on his experiences in various Nazi concentration camps.

Frankl describes his understanding: that which defines us is not about *what's happening* as much *how we respond to what's happening*. To make this point from different angles, here are several of his quotations:

> "Everything can be taken from a man but one thing: the last of human freedoms—to choose one's attitude in any given set of circumstances, to choose one's own way."
>
> "When we are no longer able to change a situation, we are challenged to change ourselves."
>
> "Between stimulus and response there is a space. In that space is our power to choose our response. In our response lies our growth and our freedom."

His is a powerful perspective. It's the difference between responding to external circumstances as the object of our singular focus vs. responding to what is inspired through us via the circumstance. Said another way: what the event ignites within us as possibility, option or choice.

This enlightened awareness contains an inherent choice point; an option with the greatest seed of all-potential. It is literally the moment of sovereignty remembered. We have the power to choose and when we do, regardless of external circumstance, new possibilities and potentialities begin to materialize into form. A mysterious, ancient force meets us and something shifts toward Divine coalescence; matter begins to shape.

In answer to the heart's undeniable clarion call toward making our unique contributions, the answer is a resounding YES: one can make a difference... just like Frankl did; just like you do.

Our defining moment is now. Deliberate choosing to act is the path. Regardless of what we are doing, how we are doing it, or if we doubt the impact of our actions, right now we can sanction our best efforts as enough. In doing so, it is ours to simply continue taking action to sustain the momentum.

The way forward is to hold the bigger vision—the macro. We can't allow ourselves to fall into the trap of getting overwhelmed, and questioning why and how we act toward creating life that works for all life—the micro. We must simply act.

As we show up—whether courageous, wrecked or unsure—and willingly enact those inspirations that come from within our deepest wisdom, we inevitably ally with others on their own journeys as they do the same. Our best efforts, met with the best efforts of others, make this planet wide movement that much more potent and powerful.

❧ PART 4 ❧

# *Tools*

## FOR

# REVERENT
# ENGAGEMENT

# 9

# WE AMPLIFY

(Sande Hart)

---

**We Amplify** Our Yes By Listening Out and In
as inspired by a conversation with Sande Hart

---

TAKE A LOOK at the past 20 years of your life. Like many women, you may wonder *how in the world did I get here?* Sande is no different. *How did she* fall into the industry of women's empowerment, of peace building, of community building, of creating distinct projects and initiatives that are actually showing resiliency and sustainability?

For Sande, she learned to continually say Yes to life's invitations with practice in using a few potent tools that paved her way forward.

One tool she distinctly remembers is learning the sacred art of *listening out* and *listening in*. Some experience *listening out* and *listening in* as an activation in and of itself because together, they comprise an efficient and harmonious, closed system of give/take, inflow/outflow, etc.

When we *listen out* in service to another, an attunement occurs. This aspect of the dynamic process gives the other an opportunity to hear themselves, provides a safe container for them to become more authentic, and potentially cracks open something new for them to experience and explore.

In the act of *listening out* with true compassion and attentiveness, there is an inherent gift for us, too; the ability to *listen in*. To *listen in* gives us access to *our own* signals, information, wisdom and guidance based on the energies that underlie what is being spoken by the other—the energies of the actual words. These are heard or felt within our emotional and physical bodies. Think: call and response. A signal goes out (the stirrings that originate by the act of listening to the other) and that results in a tangible response that lands in our own system.

As Sande immersed herself in the practice of truly listening to others and herself, she tapped into a new frequency of hearing. It's one thing to listen. It's another to actually hear the message beyond language and respond in what she ultimately described as "her calling."

She began recognizing when opportunities or creative ideas appeared and sparkled around her. Without the gift of *listening out* and *listening in*, it would have been easy to just dismiss them or think *I don't have what it takes to do anything about that*. Can't we all relate?

When an idea landed in her field, it always felt inspired. She noticed distinct stopping points where there was nothing to do but address the task immediately in front of her, such as creating a website as the container for her fresh idea. She took just the next step. And that was her way of saying Yes to her calling. As she describes it, "The key tool in getting to the point where I said Yes over and over again was the listening, but the actual mechanism to keep me there was trust, faith, confidence and most of all, courage." We've all stood at the precipice of our own grand becoming— that point of knowing we need to take a leap. And not just once, but many times throughout a lifetime.

This approach of saying Yes is scary if we allow ourselves to think about it too much. Yet, it's calming to remember that we can lean into our faith and trust in the calling itself. Our internal GPS is an infallible guide.

Our Yes is the arc between recognizing the call and doing something about it. Our Yes, our attention, bridges our calling with a tangible action that births it into physical form.

It's helpful to remember that action is not always about moving in the specific direction originally inspired. Our discernment might lead us to saying a series of smaller Yeses that take us on a meandering path. Yet even that is still saying Yes to the over-arching call. Action is our acknowledgement: *I hear you. I hear the calling. I'm willing to step off into the unknown or take this on if it's in alignment with my highest and deepest visions*, which brings us back to the art of *listening out* and *listening in*. One cannot *answer* the call if they cannot first clearly feel or hear the call. And there's benefit to so many when we do.

When we say Yes within our own circles of influence, we vicariously give license to those who don't yet have the clarity or courage to show up with their own Yes... yet! Generally speaking, as women we tend to discount our value and our inspirations. We automatically think: *I don't have what it takes*. But, as Marianne Williamson stated with such clarity and authority:

> *Our deepest fear is not that we are inadequate. Our deepest fear is that we are powerful beyond measure. It is our light, not our darkness, that most frightens us. We ask ourselves, 'Who am I to be brilliant, gorgeous, talented, fabulous?' Actually, who are you not to be?*

To further grow trust in saying Yes, another mighty tool Sande used began as a game with her children. She elaborates, "When my kids were little, my husband and I had so much fun giving them their presents in creative ways. And some of our favorites were to send them on a scavenger hunt. As an example, they'd wake up to find the end of a long piece of yarn nearby, which they had to follow all around the house. I'd weave the yarn throughout every room. I'd go back to rooms that had already been "woven." I'd go in this thing and out that thing. It would take him a half an hour or so to follow the thread, yet finally they'd find a surprise. It was so fun!

"The yarn in this story is symbolic for us trusting that there's always *something* on the other end of the following the spiritual thread. Even though I am never sure what, exactly, is at the end, just knowing, trusting, having faith and confidence, and courage that it will lead me to my very next Yes, is a richness I carry throughout the adventure. The Universe is infinite in its delightful surprises."

Following our Yes rarely goes how we envision. Most of us want to take a beeline, going directly from Point A to Point B in the shortest amount of time. While it helps to start with a strategic plan—because that provides an overall structure—you stick to the plan only as long as that's inspired. And even if you end up making a 180-degree change-in-direction, you do it because you know that's now the path you know you're supposed to be on.

Just like following a physical thread, often we're guided to places we never could imagine at first, but are essential to our journey (and mostly recognized in hindsight). That's how we build strong muscles and learn all kinds of lessons along the way, adding to what we already know. While a meandering path may not be what we plan, it *is* always interesting and a practice in refining our skills of subtle discernment. Ultimately, it's about being willing to listen and act upon what wants to happen in the immediate. The path will be revealed because our Yeses have an inherent momentum that requires only our attention, devotion, and curiosity.

So, pick up the end of the thread in front of you and

follow it with childlike delight toward your intended surprise. The Universe wants for you what you cannot even imagine and will manage the details of getting you there. Your job is to *listen out* in service to others, *listen in* in service to your calling and say a big, fat Yes to what follows next.

# WE CREATE

## (Sura Kim)

---

**We Create** Whole, Harmonized Meditation Practices
as inspired by a conversation with Sura Kim

---

THE DIVINE FEMININE is an integral part of meditation. However, most meditation traditions were founded, evolved and disseminated from the masculine perspective, which emphasized mental concentration and discipline using strong willpower.

Universally, male energy is recognized as godlike. And there's a reason for that. In an effort to connect to God, people personified God and divine consciousness according to cultural conditioning.

In the early days of yoga, patriarchal rule dictated that only men were permitted to practice yoga, pursue spiritual practice, and explore enlightenment. Created by men for men, from there, yogic techniques, styles and traditions shaped modern religions and spiritual practices. Therefore, faiths refer to God as "him." But by upholding and supporting that through our traditions, it subconsciously and unconsciously imprints the collective over and over again to a lop-sided orientation. What is inherently missing in today's meditative practices is the inclusion of a soft, effortless, feminine energy.

Much of what we've learned about meditation is that feminine modalities are separate from the actual practice. When in reality—especially when harnessed for magical and healing arts—they are obvious elements of a *holistic* meditative practice. At its best, meditation is a spiritual, whole energy health system of heart (feminine) *and* mind (masculine).

If the goal of meditation is to develop a sound spiritual practice that opens a pathway to the higher vibrations and dimensions of our consciousness, that's not possible without the inclusion of the feminine frequency. When we have the courage to do that, we gain access to the power of surrender, the willingness to let go of control, the trusting of life's mysteries, and the ability of truly loving and nurturing ourselves.

Surrendering to that harmonized sweet spot within ourselves reflects the might of something gentle. It reveals our inner softness, and the openness and willingness to be vulnerable to the Universe and the Divine within ourselves, and others. Instead of forcing ourselves to meditate, we can immerse ourselves in gentle self-care, as we learn and mature our practice.

What often happens in masculine-based approaches is the intent to *bypass human emotion and feeling*. In some meditation traditions, we're even discouraged from engaging the imagination, as it's considered a secondary or nonsensical aspect of meditation to transcend. Discarded as insignificant, unimportant, irrelevant. Yes, that is the underlying message: transcend your feelings, transcend your emotions, transcend your mind, and transcend imagination. Essentially, transcend being human.

Several traditions even teach body transcendence, but the physical body was never meant to be transcended. It's what holds the Spirit. And it is only when we are fully and wholly present in the body that it can be used for embodying true spiritual realization. We lose exponentially when we shun or bypass the body. It exists to inform. By loving and listening to the body's wisdom, it serves as a reliable guide toward enlightenment.

In the evolution of meditation itself, right now we're in the delicate process of taking everything that's traditional about meditation, and flipping it around completely, because there's a whole other side to it.

Meditation is so many things. And a meditative practice can be so much more with the inclusion of feminine energies.

In its most pristine state, meditation is about vibration. It's about being conscious, intentional, and deliberate. Meditation helps us raise and expand our consciousness. When we're in an expanded state of consciousness, we can harness and direct our lifeforce energy towards creating good, utilizing it toward healing, or manifesting blessings. As we amass lifeforce energy within, we naturally feel more alive, vital and connected to all-that-is.

> **MEDITATION** is a catalyst for creating magic, and flow, and synchronicity, and possibility.
>
> **MEDITATION** is learning how to create alchemy through the process of discovery.
>
> **MEDITATION** is healing medicine.
>
> **MEDITATION** is a transformative experience and process.

Meditation is about having a full heart awakening and coming into contact with your true self. And that is only possible by granting feminine energy permission to flow freely and loosen the tough, rigid layers of conditioning, with unconditional love and grace.

It's our time to experience what's on the other side of balancing softness with the structure of discipline. The zero point between gentleness and love, and structure and discipline, is a holistic, harmonized, spiritual meditative practice that's alive and ever in-motion toward our greatest expressions as love-beings.

Full, holistic meditation is the creative feminine integrated into a basic masculine meditation practice; the synergistic magic of what the feminine and masculine energies can be when they are equally valued, incorporated and calibrated for the infinite possibilities available to us in New Earth.

# 11

# WE WIELD

(Lauren Tatarsky)

---

**We Wield** Rarified Anger as the
Embodied Energy of Fiery Passion
as inspired by a conversation with Lauren Tatarsky

---

THERE IS NO shortage of mythological stories and imagery portraying females full of rage. Durga, Kali and Lilith come to mind. With a very wide brush-stroke, a patriarchal picture has been painted about goddesses who dare to express as anything other than motherly, gentle, demure, submissive, obedient, or subservient to the status quo. Even with their fury justified—social injustice, as only one example—they are demoralized and demonized. And that, in itself, is enough to infuriate anyone.

Worshipped by Hindus throughout India and Nepal, Kali is among the most demonized of all Goddesses. Known as the destroyer of evil forces, she causes destruction for the purpose of protecting the innocent. She fights evil with her signature fiery passion. She's not nice about it. She's not pretty about it. And she doesn't hold back. She's blue and her tongue is hanging out. Underfoot is her beloved, Shiva, and she's… just… gone… wild. Uncompromising and unapologetic, Kali's business is to get on with slaying and she knows it.

Yet, as her story evolves, she is brought to a pivotal moment of self-awareness and realization. She does all this powerful, good work to protect innocent lives, but it gets away from her. It turns into something she's not in control of anymore and she stops just before killing Shiva, her lover. The moral of the story? Unchecked anger causes us to stray from the pure intent of our origins, lose our vision and our footing, and leaves destruction in our wake. Not quite the legacy we had in mind!

Kali's mythological narrative delivers the message that it is a great responsibility to wield anger in ultimate service to goodness. And that that is only possible when we direct its energy for the highest good according to a Divine definition and rarified expression.

Otherwise, we are left singed, or worse, scorched beyond recognition.

## Early Onset

As with all early learning, we learn about anger from those around us. In concentric circles from there, our base understanding is reinforced by larger influences; cultural, societal and institutional. By the time we reach adulthood, we have seen many distorted examples of anger whether repressed or suppressed, or explosive, aggressive and violent. Their unconscious anger patterns, or our own variations, have become, or inform, ours.

To be a part of familial, cultural or societal groups, early adaptation of their norms is literally a survival skill. And while denying or repressing anger can be an essential adaptation to early experiences, yet there is a cost: we end up moving through life with a distorted understanding of anger, and seethe within or explode without. We misunderstand anger's power, its true, beautiful, pure essence, and its purpose. We are foreign to its ability to galvanize and harmonize when wielded with mastery of Self. And instead we enact and perpetuate anger's lowest frequencies simply because no one taught us or modeled differently for us.

When that realization eventually lands, often in adulthood, it does so with a heavy thud. No longer willing to be complacent and implode or explode due to unconscious patterning or everyday circumstance, we know we have work ahead. This time it's building a rapport with the energy of fiery passion named *anger*. Babes on this journey, there's much to learn about using anger's fiery passion with purpose. But first let's make this important distinction...

## Anger Distorted, Anger Rarified

⋈ **Anger** is a single stream with two expressions: distorted or rarified.

⋈ **Distorted anger**... we've all seen it. We may have even perpetuated it. Repressed or suppressed, explosive, aggressive or violent, this expression is often used to manipulate, dominate or control. It is reactive. It is over-reactive. It is marked by high emotion and  uncharacteristic behavior. Distorted anger can smolder for years or decades. Distorted anger can flash and recede just as quickly. It is unpredictable.

Anger in its distorted form is that which has morphed from rarified anger into something harmful, erratic and extreme, without useful application and causing only damage.

✷ **Rarified anger**... few of us have seen this expression modeled with mastery, yet this is how it looks. It is responsive, not reactive. It is directed in service to positive change. It is measured and appropriately-responsive to current circumstance. It extends no reach to the past to inform the current moment. It is fully-present. It is strategic, calculated and focused. Its outlet is reserved for the perfect moment, delivering maximum impact. It possesses an inherent wisdom that informs its user, whose directive is to use its power for goodness. Ego/mind disengages as rarified anger moves *through* the physical body.

Anger in its rarified form is that which is a catalyst for change. After any initial upheaval brought about by anger's higher expression, it is ultimately useful, helpful, and beneficial to bringing increased awareness and creative inspiration to shift the status quo.

## Rarified Anger Embodied

Psychological studies show that anger is often an undiagnosed indicator of depression and repressed grief (distorted anger) that needs healing and retraining toward healthy expression (rarified anger).

When we feel anger not as an unresolved emotion (distorted) but as the energy of fiery passion in our bodies (rarified), something important shifts. We begin to move in collaboration with it as the pure energy stream it is and discover how to hold healthy boundaries around self-worth, clarity, action and fiery passion. And as we establish and vitalize a more intimate relationship with fiery passion, we gain access to the power of its healthy and conscious uses toward righteous thought and action.

Anger is held in our lower chakras. And in most aspects of patriarchy, as women we are severed from our lower chakras because they are our power centers and that does not serve the patriarchal agenda. Yet, reclaiming the energy of anger gets us back in our bodies in a deeply-healing way. Embodiment is an act of deliberate reclamation of our lower chakras, allowing us to become whole again and take action from that wholeness.

## Anger as the Energy of Fiery Passion

Instead of repressing, suppressing, exploding, aggressing or violenting anger, we can choose differently which is the key to our aliveness and our sense of Self. Fiery passion is precisely what we need to make wise decisions, establish clear boundaries, and take action in our lives. It's also the key to making positive change in our world because the two—micro and macro—are mirrored in each other.

We often perpetuate patriarchal patterns simply because we aren't tapped into our own passionate awareness. So, using anger as the catalytic fuel for rectifying imbalance and injustice on our block or across the world becomes an essential skill as we look toward the future. Anger helps us to recognize and respond to what needs to shift so we can create the world in which we actually *want* to live.

Fire is apt symbolism for these times. Often referred to as a "force of nature," fire is commonly seen as destructive, yet it also comprises instructive aspects; those beneficial qualities that can only emerge by fire's initiations.

However justified, anger takes only one of two forms: mastered or unmastered. May the "demonized" goddesses of fire and fury have free reign in you, as you allow embodied, rarified anger to inform and direct your path, and express with purity and potency.

# 12

## WE WEAVE

(Sara Jamil)

---

**We Weave** a Global Web of Connection
with Essence-to-Essence Conversation
as inspired by a conversation with Sara Jamil

---

CONVERSATION is the way of New Earth, but not as we've previously known it. Essence to essence communication is the path forward. It's how the Divine Mother and Divine Feminine come through, into form. And we all know how crucial that is right now.

At their very essence, these healing conversations begin with trusting the voice from within, which is a skill of its own.

Through societal conditioning, we have become accustomed to the status quo in our exchanges with others. We force experience through that tiny eye of a needle to conform to our conditioned expectations. In doing so, we diminish what's ultimately possible in connection with others, and our experiences can only ever be contracted and one dimensional. What we learn we perpetuate, without knowing there's a way to connect that's much more gratifying.

When we are at ease with each other and comfortable enough to be vulnerable, that's when essence to essence conversation and connection is possible.

These interactions begin by letting down one's guard, and speaking and listening from the place of *I truly see you, I truly feel you, I truly hear you.* When the other person feels that trust, they feel safe enough to show up fully. Sitting together in the safety and support of that space opens the energy. And alchemy follows; two energies uniting and birthing a third energy that nurtures everyone involved.

Essence to essence conversations contain an inherent guiding wisdom that knows precisely how to lead us through... *if* we are willing to follow that lead. When we do, we always go somewhere unexpected and exhilarating, in a characteristically feminine, meandering way.

The potential for essence to essence connection is in each of us (individually), all of us (collectively) and everywhere (all the physical and energetic spaces in-between). Whether walking alone in a forest (and therefore in direct communion with nature) or interacting with others (and in direct communication human-to-human) it's up to us to intensify our desire to explore its many facets. When we do, it naturally grows and takes on a life of its own.

Essence to essence, together we are weaving a tight-knit web of women across the world. We have something invaluable to offer each other. We can't just sit in our own little home, community, or country. We need to uphold each other through the variety of experiences life offers by talking, listening, speaking and connecting, and doing that while anchored in our own signature essence.

How does that look in everyday life?

Nurture the connections you make though simple day to day interactions. Follow whatever prompts land in your awareness. Reach out after initial contact is made just to check in. Offer to be a part of what another is creating.

So often when we make contact, we want something for ourselves. When you extend yourself to another in support of moving *them* toward achieving *their* vision, you will be remembered. Propel others with your skill set, enthusiasm or simply, your interest. It can be the seemingly smallest gesture, yet it can mean so much to the recipient. If nothing else, it shows them they're not alone. Again, this makes you stand out from the crowd.

This web we create with hands extended is what holds us up both individually and on a collective level. Every little thing that you do in your circle of care—whether in your home, family or community—has an impact. Our actions, however seemingly small or insignificant, set the butterfly effect in motion. The impact doesn't end in our immediate environment. It ripples and ripples far beyond our visibility and awareness, even circling back around to us in ways we wouldn't necessarily even know is because of us. We don't need proof that the seed we plant has impact. We can simply carry the knowing that it does and let that continue to grow incentive and momentum as we carry on with the business of life.

How often do we have the thought *I wish I could do something*, which is immediately followed by *How am*

*I going to do it?* Each us has been there. It's easy to get overwhelmed by leading with the question. When we hold the knowing that whatever actions we take will have a positive impact, our view shifts. No longer focused on the *how*, opportunities naturally present themselves.

As you embody and enact the thought *a better world starts with me*, that has tremendous power. It's simple and yet has a direct application in every conversation, in every connection, in every interaction. It also reverberates through our everyday awareness, meditations, and prayers. As sentient beings, we are continually emitting signals that carry impact in many meaningful ways in potent little packages. Sending prayers to those we don't yet know, but will some day as part of our path, or holding a heightened frequency that our intentions are landing in the lives of others in tangible ways, are acts of building the web of unification and connectedness. Our personal and private spiritual practices paired with outward action make a real difference.

In connections and communications of this caliber—with each of us investing our unique contribution—we can truly see each other, honor each other and help one another's work. Yet, creating a global sisterhood doesn't mean that we're all going to be together at the same time, have the same interests or passions, or even be in connection long term. It's more that in every moment of now we hold something in common: a global vision of inner- and inter-connectedness paved by essence to essence reflection.

We know how to do this. We know it from birth. We are hard wired to nurture, to support, and to connect. Essence to essence, we join hands and hearts, and thereby build bridges through communication. As women, it's what we innately do so well and how Divine Mother and Divine Feminine come through us and into form.

# *Essence-to-Essence Conversation*

## SPEAKER

1. Move attention inward.

2. Maintain focus on your inner voice.

3. Say exactly what you want to say
   without judgement or censorship.

4. Stop speaking when you are complete.

## LISTENER

1. Focus fully on the speaker.

2. Extend and maintain loving, accepting attention to speaker.

3. Listen without judgement or interruption.

4. Relinquish agenda.

5. Refrain from polite or courteous responses.

6. Move into speaker role when speaker is clearly finished.

7. Follow four speaker guidelines.

# 13

# WE CIRCLE

(Ann Smith)

---

**We Circle** in Action

as inspired by a conversation with Ann Smith

---

THERE IS A sacredness to circle. The shape itself connotes equality among its participants. Everyone in circle is seen as a leader, a facilitator, a listener, a weaver of the collective wisdom and collective creativity.

Circle acclimates women to being valued, validated, and empowered. In the safe environment of circle, every participant is provided the opportunity to learn and practice the skill of listening without judgment.

In most conversational exchanges, we are prone to listening just enough to formulate a response. Thoughts constantly run through our heads. This isn't truly listening. Instead of thinking about what to say, everyone in circle is actively listening and supporting the one speaking to emerge into a greater authentic expression through the process. This way of connecting is deeper than most people think possible before experiencing it for themselves.

Circle allows women to be in the same space physically where they can look into one another's eyes and lean in energetically to hear on multiple levels. *Every* voice is heard and deeply felt by those listening. And there is a freshness to every moment—as if something new is being birthed with each addition to the communal cauldron. What's being shared is a new thought and a new feeling which changes the concoction into something that's never existed before.

Speaking in circle requires expressing straight from the heart, which only enhances its beauty and potency. The experience is truly magical and the value is spiritual, physical, intellectual, and emotional. It draws us into engaging on a higher plane than our usual everyday interactions.

And for those who think circle is reserved for the rare occasion or strictly ceremonial purpose, inherently it contains no such limitation. Anytime, anywhere, circle provides the experience itself, and everyone involved, all the life giving nutrients needed for something new, something healing, something exciting, and just the right something needed for the greater good.

Circle is simultaneously ancient and modern. It comes from our ancestors, who from the very beginning of time, gathered around the fire and told stories. Through the art of story telling, elders and youngers shared tales of the beautiful harmony between the Divine Feminine and the Divine Masculine. Sadly, this heavenly construct was eventually lost... forbidden and hidden for thousands of years. Patriarchy ruled. Power over eclipsed power with. Yet... circle is the definitive medicine needed to replace patriarchy, which at its foundation, divides people and positions them as adversaries instead of allies.

The Great Illumination is happening now... and it's extraordinary. We are definitively accomplishing what was once deemed impossible. The Divine Feminine is being revealed in books, poems, prayers, music, and videos. She is emerging in wild and wonderful ways and circle plays a part. After all, circle is known to birth new worlds.

When we speak of the Divine Feminine while encircled by other women, we affirm one another in our own personal divinity, as well as the spirit of the collective Divine Feminine. And that's the celebration. That's the excitement. That's when women amass the courage to do amazing things in the world... a world that doesn't have a clue what we're talking about. Yet, *we* do, and that's all that matters.

In intimate groups of shared leadership—circle-by-circle—we attain a higher consciousness. Each circle that forms is evidence of the phenomena of the morphic field. And we know in our hearts we're connected across the world because there is no such thing as separation. In circle, every one is equally valued and equally shares vital information.

It's a rich, mutual exchange of information, no matter the age or culture. In circle, one can learn in a very short period of time. Things just change, time stops and all of a sudden, you're transformed because you've been transported into a different realm of learning and being with one another.

Being in circle also transports us into a different dimension which is very different than chronological time. In sacred circle, simply allowing the process—which is divine—is the guide which moves you into Kairos time where everything somehow gets done that needs to be done. We just need to go with the flow, which in itself is divinity.

Letting go and trusting that the flow will naturally lead, doesn't mean we aren't scared sometimes of the uncertainty involved in merely showing up. We are conditioned to think we need to bring something more—that what we have isn't enough. And that's only human, but be assured: everything needed will appear for us to nestle into the circle process and experience all that's there for us.

The circle process gives us access to understanding each other on a deeper level, because the commonality we have as women is already there… as mothers, as caretakers, and as people who care for the community and understand what universal love is about. And that may be the definition of heaven on earth. It is the ideal. Circle is the rare place where we know we are truly loved and accepted, and where we can be our very best selves.

Circle is also the most dangerous thing there is to patriarchy (and the patriarchy doesn't even know it)! Circle seems like a benign activity. Because the concept, and women, and the Divine Feminine are not valued, the establishment doesn't have a clue about how perfectly circle is poised to shift our future. It is the invisible force that will eclipse patriarchy with a whole new choice of how to be with one another in a way that serves us all.

## Circle—A Construct For Planetary Transformation?

It's not as if we have to fight against anything. That's resistance. We just have to be who we are meant to be—to blossom into that. As women we are compelled to gather and use circle principles with the deep listening, the deep caring, and the deep understanding we already possess. By doing that, we are changing the world. When we value ourselves, the Divine Feminine and circle, there's absolutely no stopping the momentum developed by those conjoined forces.

The initiation rituals of lighting a candle, silence, music, prayers, or singing opens the portal. Through that portal is universal flow. You're the allowing. The heart self relaxes, magnetizing magic because the two—heart and magic—occupy the same frequency. Everyone participating will do what's necessary to make it a beautiful experience because at some early point in the circle process, the group has become one-pulse.

For a moment see what a contrast that is to the events of our everyday lives! How often have people been in a setting where they felt judged and then self-conscious around that or worried about what they're going to say? Most of us have spent a lot of time there, so we can relate. Now, imagine relaxing fully into being yourself. And being completely supported in doing that!

None of us becomes our higher or best selves, by ourselves. It happens in circle, whether that's in a more formal, ritualized encounter or a less structured experience. We express from our divine nature in circle process. And we each play a crucial role in that. Each part will be different, yet all the parts are needed... especially if we're joining for a common task—doing something together that requires a variety of skills and passions. Everyone can participate based on their own interests, strengths, and their own willingness to follow through based on the larger vision. Power with rather than power over = we all thrive.

The power given to us is the power from whatever we call our source; God, the universe, the divine, spirit, etc. It is an unlimited spiritual power. And just like creativity, everybody has access to it. And accessing it is for the higher good, not for the benefit of the individual. The individual benefit is that we get to live our purpose.

When we act in circle, in dynamism with others toward a common intent or accomplishment, we are living out our potential, we are being loved, and we're in a community that is connected on a heart level. And we know that being in community is one of the healthiest things we can do as human beings.

Ann Smith passionately shares, "You can see why I'm a circle evangelist. When I heard Margaret J. Wheatley talk about living systems, and how all life moves towards the light and towards the energy, I thought *that's all we have to remember*. We don't need complicated roles because we naturally self organize into the necessary roles that need to be filled. They're not assigned by another. They don't need to be. The alchemy of circle is an example of a vibrant, living process. Circle is a self organizing system. Informed by its wisdom, we know what needs to be done and we just get on with it. Everybody gets to be a part. That's what I see when women work together.

"For example, a group of women and I gathered in circle for a weekend workshop. For that time, the rented apartment we shared was home. Activities included preparing for a party. We worked together so beautifully. I see that whenever there's a gathering of women and there are tasks to be done. It's so organic. Everybody just pitches in and does their part. It's almost like watching a dancer or an orchestra. And it's interesting. The thought that comes to mind is *a circle process in action*.

"In preparation for the party, everybody got to do what they wanted and needed to do. That was a circle. We didn't know how many people were coming and it didn't matter. We each simply performed the aspect that resonated most with us as individuals. Without a plan and without a lead orchestrator, it worked flawlessly. And that was even true with the workshop. People were setting up chairs and then others pitched in, and together we got everything done.

"Another example is my wonderful friend Martha, who is a Mayan priestess from Guatemala. I had no idea, but she planned a 5-minute ceremony. I didn't think it could happen in such a brief time because I've attended similar ceremonies. They last for hours. In spite of my initial doubts, Martha said, "Ann, I can do it." That's all I needed. And as it turned out, those 5 minutes were unbelievably powerful.

"My relationship with circle began by finding a circle, which lead to starting a circle myself and diving into the flow because it's just so magnificent. There are a lot of circle organizations now. It's happening all over the world and it's only going to grow—exponential expansion of the global circle, the global hug that embraces us all," Ann proclaims.

There's a primal need not only to be a part of a group, but to be heard. To do that we have to slow down. We have to create safe environments. And we have to really listen to each other. The spirit of circle now invites us to go beyond its original framework. It beckons us to insert its principles into every interaction as we go about the business of our everyday lives.

No longer reserved to sitting in sacred circle in the traditional sense, we can look directly into the eyes of the grocery cashier, drug addict, barista, homeless person or auto mechanic and energetically hand that person the "talking stick" as we bear witness. In doing so, we silently grant that person permission to speak freely with their full authority, while we fully-presence and listen with rapt attention and intrigue at what is about to be added to the cauldron of life.

## Circle-in-circle—concentric circles

Circle-upon-circle—circle-strata. There is nothing more inherently feminine than circle. The shape itself. The spirals circle inspires. The sitting circle. The experience. The Divine Feminine weaves in her mystical, circuitous way. While one cannot follow logically, at the heart of circle, is circle spirit, wanting to expand through circle in action.

## PART 5

# WHAT HAPPENS
# WHEN WOMEN
# *Play*

# 14

W ITH SO MUCH urgency pressing in from all directions, it's easy to get caught in the seriousness of these times and stay there. Yet, levity is a powerful mechanism that supports us in sustaining our Earth loving actions. Taking breaks for fun is imperative in this long-game.

Most of us were raised with the WASP (White Anglo-Saxon Protestant) values. Work is good. Play is bad. "Idle hands are the devil's workshop." Effort is admirable. Performance (especially academic) is commended. So much so, that we have removed art, recess, and sports from school curriculum.

There are no awards or mass approval for those who play well. We tolerate it in children. Sometimes we even envy or resent it in them. We know how to play as children, but then we grow up and we are required to leave behind the land of play. Sadly, there is a cost.

When we do this what do we leave behind? We leave behind the experience of living fully, joyfully, creatively, in the moment, and connecting internally to whatever we want to express.

The energy of play plugs us fully into the present moment. How can we possibly play well when we are thinking about the past or projecting into the future? It can't happen. Play can only exist in the NOW.

Having been a parentified child who moved into a sense of responsibility too early and focusing on looking good and pleasing others, I learned to abandon the moment, attempting to control the future and escape the past. This way of living robbed me of my rightful endowment of the capacity to play.

I received the unexpected gift of the ability to communicate with my sister Nene after she transitioned from this life. I learned experientially, which was the only way I could receive the words coming from my own inner listening. Hearing was only possible by being fully and completely present. The experience became a vehicle for re-establishing my ability to remain in the present. My motivation was high.

As I write and reflect, I notice the words *present* and *connection* appearing consistently. I stay in the moment and listen internally. What comes is that play is a connection with the self in the moment expressed through creativity.

This is where we are now as evolutionary humans. We are evolving, expressing, growing, and expanding through play. We are releasing the old way of trudging laboriously through the heavier, denser, lower vibrations. Play is the energy of the New Earth. Powerful, focused, expressive play. The higher vibrations we are living in support this capacity.

Ask yourself: How do you plug into the energy of play? What is your capacity for play? How can you grow it?

# EPILOGUE

THERE IS NO EXPERIENCE like writing a book. It is a process of gathering pieces together that come from within me, from the outside world, and from within others. As a psychotherapist and spiritual seeker, my primary focus has been my inner world, inviting out and supporting the inner worlds of others.

The creation of *What Happens When Women Converge* has been a profound collaboration of the wisdom of the extraordinary women I interviewed who each shared their unique understanding of their role in the collective feminine.

In her process of editing the book, Charlon's ethereal crafting of the interviews revealed the essence of each conversation. Her process felt to me like watching her sift for diamonds, polish them, and present them in an exquisite setting.

These, combined with the messages I received from my reverent engagement with Mother Earth, created an offering that feels more like an energetic vortex than a simple book.

As a book-lover most of my life, I have discovered that as we evolve spiritually, the energy of the written word is so much more than words on paper. Books can be an energetic container that offers the reader a shift into another level of consciousness. My belief and wish is that this book provides that acceleration and deepening that Charlon and I experienced ourselves in its creation.

# AUTHOR BIO

**PATRICIA FERO** was born for these times. Her life is dedicated to igniting the collective feminine toward planetary awakening. Her capacity for clearing her own internalized patriarchy and fierce listening are the magic she brings to every setting.

She is the author of five nonfiction books—*Mining for Diamonds; What Happens When Women Wake Up? Sacred Marching Orders*; and *The Other Side of the Door.*

She also writes passionately about "Fierce Listening" as a strategy to restore and strengthen human connections weakened by our increasing focus on various screens and "all things electronic."

Patrica maintains an active psychotherapy practice in Ann Arbor, Michigan assisted by her black cocker spaniel, Dexter who pretends he is a therapy dog. She holds a Masters Degree in Social Work from the University of Michigan.

Marianne Williamson has praised
Patricia's work by saying:

"Women owning our power and using it collaboratively
is what our planet desperately needs."